Look, Look! I Wrote a Book!

Reproducible **LITTLE BOOKS** for Emergent Readers

By **Linda Ball** and **Laurel Brucker**

Illustrated by Vickey Bolling

Good Year Books

An Imprint of Addison-Wesley Educational Publishers, Inc.

Acknowledgments

With thanks to the community
of learners at Metcalf
Laboratory School, whose
support and enthusiasm
continue to inspire us.

LB & LB

 Good Year Books

are available for most basic curriculum subjects plus many
enrichment areas. For more Good Year Books, contact your
local bookseller or educational dealer. For a complete catalog
with information about other Good Year Books, please write:

Good Year Books
1900 East Lake Avenue
Glenview, Illinois 60025

Book Design by Lynne F. Grenier
Text Copyright © 1998 Linda Ball and Laurel Brucker.
Illustrations Copyright © 1998 Good Year Books.
All Rights Reserved.
Printed in the United States of America.

ISBN 0-673-36357-0

4 5 6 7 8 9 - CRK - 06 05 04 03 02 01 00 99

Table of Contents

Preface

We created these little books to fill a void we had in our literacy program. Our classrooms were filled with print and many examples of children's work. Our classroom libraries were stocked with excellent fiction and nonfiction literature. We had adequate collections of small books at the emergent level. Yet, our children were not always able to find books they could read successfully at an independent level.

We also felt that it was important for children to have opportunities to write creatively. We have always provided many occasions for writing and encouraged our children to write and illustrate their own books. We wanted all of the children to have their own collection of books that they could take home and practice reading with their families. The little books included in *Look, Look, I Wrote a Book!* became the perfect solution to our literacy concerns, providing many opportunities for the children to practice their reading and writing skills. We have found that children enjoy the repetition and predictable language in these little books, and they love the way they can personalize the books with their own ideas, words, and illustrations.

These little books are easily integrated into a curriculum, to reinforce a concept or skill, extend literature, or support a theme. Notice that on p.12 we have included a Skills Organization Chart so you can easily see which skills are reinforced in each little book.

Children are excited when they see a favorite song, poem, or story in the little book form. The text that they have already learned from a chart or big book becomes part of a little book that they can read, write, and illustrate on their own. As the children begin to collect the little books, the question frequently asked is "Will we get our own little book like that?" Their enthusiasm for the little books has gone far beyond our expectations!

The addition of the share-and-sign page at the end of each book is the incentive many children need to motivate them to read to others. We ask that the children read their book to at least three others, and we are pleased to find that they often draw additional lines so they can read to even more friends. Their enthusiasm is contagious! We are thrilled to see the carry-over when children begin to add share-and-sign lines to other books that they have created in our writing centers.

To help our beginning writers, we exhibit word charts to help them experience more success. We also provide word walls in our classroom where we keep an ongoing list of words pertaining to our units of study. In addition, we keep pictionaries, dictionaries, and resource books readily available as other tools in the writing process. We encourage the children to use whatever print is accessible and always accept and encourage their independent writing attempts. The children are eager to attempt writing in this nonthreatening environment.

We have learned through trial and error which little books are the most successful and popular. We have experimented with size, print, and format. All of the little books included here have been child tested and parent approved! Every child that has used these books has felt success toward becoming a reader. We hope that you and your children will find the little books an exciting addition to your literacy program.

Linda Ball
Laurel Brucker
Co-Authors

How to Use This Book

Look, Look! I Wrote a Book! contains reproducible little books to enhance any emergent reading program. They are versatile and easily integrated into any curriculum. These little books provide young children with many opportunities to practice reading and writing while reinforcing basic concepts, putting songs and poetry into print, and enhancing theme experiences. Printed words appear in meaningful contexts and give children an opportunity to discover the richness of language through simple, repetitive text based on oral language. The little books encompass the many stages of reading development that most emergent readers experience:

- *enjoyment* • *memorization* • *retelling of the story*
- *word recognition* • *reading the text with accuracy*

When the little books are introduced effectively and used as an integral part of a literacy program, children will replicate the reading model provided by the teacher. The rhythmical language and repetitive structure of the books encourage the children to participate and interact with the print. The little books provide opportunities for students at varying stages of reading development to experience success in a noncompetitive environment. Literacy knowledge grows through engagement with the books. The share-and-sign component fosters literacy through social interaction within the context of a community of readers and writers. In essence, the little books provide an atmosphere where all children can be successful and thereby develop a love of reading.

The little books provide an excellent means of assessing students' progress and development through the reading process. From early stages of memorization to word recognition and reading behaviors, the little books encourage the students to behave like readers. This collection of books builds on successful reading experiences, develops a positive attitude toward reading, and gives children of every ability an opportunity to enjoy reading and be successful.

How do I select an appropriate little book?

Choose a book that will enhance, extend, or reinforce a theme, concept, or skill. The Table of Contents groups the books into suggested themes or skill areas. However, many of the books could be used in multiple categories. See the Skills Organizer on p.12, which shows which skills are reinforced in each book.

How do I make a little book?

Reproduce a copy of the book for each student. Cut the pages in half horizontally and assemble according to page number. Each selection will begin with a cover and end with the share-and-sign page. Staple several times down the left-hand margin to create a book.

How do I introduce a little book?

Each reproducible book is preceded by a Teacher's Notes page, which gives the key concept, preparation instructions, tips on using the book effectively, and suggested literature. It is recommended that the little books be used after several experiences with the print. Introduce the students to the text and allow the children to respond, explore, and discover the text or concept. Several shared reading experiences with the print will enhance the students' success with their individual little books.

How do children make the little books their own?

Have children write their names on the covers of their own little books after the word "by." Then have them fill in words or numbers as prompted in the stories to personalize the stories. Children may illustrate their little books or color the borders as an in-class activity. As children read their little books to others, remind them to have their share-and-sign pages filled in by those they have read to. A share-and-sign page is found on the last page of each little book.

How should I use these little books in my classroom?

The little books can be integrated into any classroom curriculum. They bring songs and poems into print, reinforce basic concepts, and extend literature. The little books are most successfully used as culminating activities, after the children have many repeated exposures to the text or concept. The little books can be used to supplement a language arts program or as the keystone of a literature-based language arts program. Either way, the little books are an ideal tool to give children opportunities to explore language in a meaningful way and to help enhance a language-rich environment.

Why should I use these little books in my classroom?

All children want to learn to read. Any experiences with books are steppingstones to achieving that goal. As educators, we are always striving to provide students with a broader range of experiences. These little books provide each child with a personalized collection of books that offer successful experiences with reading and writing. The patterns of language and repetitive print encourage children to interact confidently and gain control of the text. This helps to develop a trust in print and security with their abilities as emergent readers.

How do I manage the little books in my classroom?

The children keep a collection of the little books in their designated containers in the classroom. Each container should be labeled with the child's name, preferably in his or her own handwriting, if legible, and decorated by the child. Possible containers include a shoe box, a cardboard mailing box, a plastic basket, or a plastic storage container. Containers should be stored in a place where they are readily available and easily accessible to the children. When the children accumulate approximately ten books in their containers, the books can be bundled and sent home with a parent letter. Refer to the sample parent letter, p.173.

How often should I introduce a little book?

The little books should be introduced routinely and as often as they can be integrated into the curriculum. Success will be enhanced by consistent experiences with the little books.

How can I facilitate the writing process using the little books?

The little books can be an excellent tool to encourage writing. They provide many opportunities for children to practice writing in a meaningful context. Several tools are recommended to create a safe, risk-free environment where students feel comfortable taking steps to practice writing. Some of the little books are accompanied by a thematic word list. These lists provide the students with words relating to the text or concept. In addition, it is recommended that a classroom environment be rich in print to establish a comfortable writing climate. Children should have access to pictionaries, word lists, charts, and labels. The children's temporary spelling can be accepted and encouraged.

How can I teach strategies and skills using the little books?

Reading is taught best when kept whole, meaningful, functional, and interesting. The little books can be a vehicle to allow children to construct relationships between oral and written language and develop important reading concepts. Effective guidance can focus on a variety of reading strategies within the context of a meaningful whole. Suggestions for strategies to focus on include:

• *directionality: left to right, top to bottom* • *differences between a letter, word, and sentence* • *spacing* • *punctuation* • *letter recognition* • *vocabulary and word recognition* • *sound-symbol relationships* • *noticing language patterns and rhymes* • *connecting sound to print* • *cloze procedure* • *integration of reading and writing* • *creative expression in context* • *use of sound-symbol relationships to encourage temporary spelling* • *developmental writing*

How can I increase the students' involvement with the little books?

Providing many opportunities for the students to read from their little books is recommended to create a sense of ownership and encourage repeated exposure to the text. A quiet reading time each day is an important element in any classroom schedule. This quiet reading time is an ideal opportunity for the children to read their little books with their peers. The little books can be used successfully in whole-group reading experiences. They can be read in unison to focus on reading behaviors or specific skill work. They can also provide opportunities for individuals to share their own ideas with the whole class. Small-group guided reading provides another excellent opportunity to increase the students' involvement with the little books.

How should the share-and-sign page be used?

The share-and-sign page is designed to encourage repeated readings of the books to peers and other willing listeners. The "author" reads the book to a friend and then requests the friend's signature on the back of the book. The share-and-sign page offers an incentive to the author to read often and to many friends.

How do I assess the students' progress?

One form of assessment is listening to individual students read. This can be done in a teacher/student reading experience or by observing two students participating in a shared reading time. In the Appendix, p. 174, is an assessment form that can provide a means for quick, simple evaluation by the teacher. It is recommended that the students' progress be assessed periodically throughout the school year.

Skills Organization Chart

	Written Expression	Rhyme	Creative Expression	Classifying	Repetition/Prediction	High-Frequency Words	Sound/Letter	Math Concepts	Color Words
Fall Leaves				●	●	●	●		●
Hello, Winter	●		●	●	●	●	●		
Spring Things	●		●	●	●	●	●		
The Four Seasons	●	●	●	●	●	●	●		
Blue Bird	●		●	●	●	●	●	●	●
Mary Wore Her Red Dress	●		●	●	●	●	●		●
I See Colors	●		●	●	●	●	●		●
The Dot Book	●	●	●		●	●	●	●	●
Apple Count		●		●		●	●	●	●
Buttons, Buttons	●	●	●	●	●	●	●	●	●
In My Home				●	●	●	●		
The Counting Way		●	●	●	●	●	●	●	●
Mr. Sun	●		●	●	●	●	●		
What Shall I Wear?	●		●	●	●	●	●		
When It Storms	●	●	●	●	●	●	●		
Rain on the Green Grass	●	●	●		●	●	●		
Hello Book	●				●	●	●		
ABC Tumble Down D	●	●	●		●	●	●		
School Days	●		●	●	●	●	●		
Good Night	●	●	●	●	●	●	●		
Mrs. Grady's Garden	●		●	●	●	●			
Bug Watch	●			●	●	●	●		
What's Alive?	●	●	●	●	●	●			
Fish Facts	●		●	●	●	●	●	●	
My Favorite Things	●		●	●	●	●	●		●
Always	●		●		●	●	●		
Guess Who	●		●	●	●	●			●
See My Family	●	●	●	●	●	●	●	●	

Look, Look! I Wrote a Book!

The Changing Seasons

Fall Leaves

Hello, Winter

Spring Things

The Four Seasons

Teacher's Notes for

Fall Leaves

Key Concept

Leaves change color in the fall.

Preparation

1. Gather theme-appropriate literature.

2. Prepare the chart or enlarged copy of the little book.

3. Duplicate the Fall thematic word list, p. 161.

4. Optional preparation activity: Have the children gather fall leaves, directing them to find at least one leaf of each color—red, yellow, brown, and orange.

5. Write the text of the little book on a large chart or prepare an enlarged copy of the little book.

Using the Book

1. Read literature selections to the class.

2. Introduce the text of the little book to the class and give many opportunities for practice, emphasizing the color words *red, yellow, brown,* and *orange.*

3. Share a copy of *Fall Leaves* with the class and discuss how to complete the book, calling attention to the color words.

4. Have children complete their books. The books may be illustrated by using crayons or markers, using real leaves to do leaf rubbings of the appropriate color, or gluing real leaves to each page.

5. Provide opportunities for the children to read their completed books to others and utilize the share-and-sign page.

Suggested Literature

Maestro, Betsy. *Why Do Leaves Change Color?* HarperCollins, 1994.

Ehlert, Lois. *Red Leaf, Yellow Leaf.* Harcourt Brace, 1991.

Fall Leaves

by _____

Brown leaves fall.

4

Leaves, leaves, on the tree.

1

Orange leaves fall.

5

Red leaves fall.

❷

Leaves, leaves, all set free.

❻

Yellow leaves fall.

I read my book to

1. _____

2. _____

3. _____

Hello, Winter

Key Concept

Characteristics of winter

Preparation

1. Gather theme-appropriate literature.

2. Prepare chart paper as follows for brainstorming words:
   Things I See in Winter:

3. Duplicate the Winter thematic word list, p. 162.

4. Write the text of the little book on a large chart or prepare an enlarged copy of the little book.

Using the Book

1. Read literature selections to the class.

2. Using the prepared chart, brainstorm with the children a list of words associated with winter.

3. Display and discuss the Winter thematic word list.

4. Share a copy of *Hello, Winter* with the class and discuss possible responses.

5. Ask children to complete their books.

6. Provide opportunities for the children to read their completed books to others and utilize the share-and-sign page.

Suggested Literature

Lewison, Wendy Cheyette. *Hello, Snow!* Putnam, 1994.

Maass, Robert. *When Winter Comes.* Holt, 1993.

Hello, Winter

by _____

Hello, _____.

Hello, _____.

1

Hello, _____.

5

Hello, _____.

Hello, winter!

Hello, _____ .

3

I read my book to

1. _____

2. _____

3. _____

7

Spring Things

Key Concept
Characteristics of spring

Preparation

1. Gather theme-appropriate literature.

2. Prepare chart paper as follows for brainstorming:
   Things I See in Spring:

3. Duplicate the Spring thematic word list, p. 163.

4. Write the text of the little book on a large chart or prepare an enlarged copy of the little book.

Using the Book

1. Read literature selections to the class.

2. Using the prepared chart, brainstorm with the children a list of things associated with spring.

3. Display and discuss the Spring thematic word list.

4. Share a copy of *Spring Things* with the class and discuss possible responses.

5. Ask children to complete their books using the words from the class chart and the thematic word list.

6. Provide opportunities for the children to read their completed books to others and utilize the share-and-sign page.

Suggested Literature

Moncure, Jane Belk. *Step into Spring*. Children's World, 1990.

Gomi, Taro. *Spring Is Here*. Chronicle Books, 1989.

Maass, Robert. *When Spring Comes*. Holt, 1994.

Spring Things

by _____

I like _____.

4

What are the things
you like about spring?

1

I like _____.

5

I like _____.

2

These are the things
I like about spring.

6

I like _____.

I read my book to

1. _____

2. _____

3. _____

The Four Seasons

Key Concept

Changes in nature are observable during the seasons.

Preparation

1. Gather theme-appropriate literature.

2. Write the text of the little book on a large chart or prepare an enlarged copy of the little book.

3. Prepare a brainstorming chart as follows to record characteristics of the four seasons.

   In Spring I See: **In Autumn I See:**

   In Summer I See: **In Winter I See:**

4. Prepare a copy of the little book for each child.

Using the Book

1. Read literature selections to the class.

2. Introduce the chart or enlarged copy of the little book.

3. Discuss characteristics of each season and record the children's ideas on the brainstorming chart.

4. Share a copy of *The Four Seasons* with the class and discuss possible responses.

5. Have children complete their books using the words from the brainstorming chart and the Fall, Winter, and Spring thematic word lists, pp.161–163.

6. On page six of the little book, ask children to indicate their favorite season by coloring in the appropriate circle.

7. Provide opportunities for the children to read their completed books to others and utilize the share-and-sign page.

Suggested Literature

Gibbons, Gail. *The Seasons of Arnold's Apple Tree.* Harcourt Brace, 1984.

Borden, Louise. *Caps, Hats, Socks and Mittens.* Scholastic, 1992.

The Four Seasons

by ______________________

It is winter,

I see ____________________________.

© Linda Ball, Laurel Brucker, Good Year Books.

It's summer—let's play ball.
It's autumn—leaves fall.
It's winter—soft, deep snow.
It's spring—flowers grow.

1

It is spring,

I see _____.

5

It is summer,

I see _____.

2

My favorite season is

◯ summer   ◯ winter

◯ autumn   ◯ spring

6

It is autumn,

I see _____.

3

I read my book to

1. _____

2. _____

3. _____

7

Colorful Colors

Blue Bird

Mary Wore Her Red Dress

I See Colors

The Dot Book

Teacher's Notes for

Blue Bird

Key Concept

Objects can be classified by color.

Preparation

1. Gather theme-appropriate literature.

2. Write the text of the little book on a large chart or prepare an enlarged copy of the little book.

3. Prepare chart paper for brainstorming, labeled as follows:
   Things that can be blue:

4. Prepare a copy of the little book for each child. As an extension, you can use the same format to teach other color words. Before copying for the class, use white tape or correction fluid to cover the word *blue* and then write over it with other color names.

Using the Book

1. Read literature selections to the class.

2. Read and review the little book story printed on chart paper. Have children circle the word *blue* on the chart.

3. Using the prepared chart, brainstorm with the class a list of things that are blue.

4. Introduce the chart or enlarged copy of the little book.

5. Share a copy of *Blue Bird* with the class and discuss possible responses.

6. Have children complete their books using the words from the class chart and their personal vocabularies. On page six of the little book, have children fill in a number in the box and then answer the question by circling "yes" or "no."

7. Provide opportunities for the children to read their completed books to others and utilize the share-and-sign page.

Suggested Literature

Gregorich, Barbara. *Sue Likes Blue.* School Zone Publishing Co., 1984.

Williams, Rozanne Lanczak. *I See Colors.* Creative Teaching Press, 1995.

Blue Bird

by _____

I see a blue _____.

Blue bird, blue bird,
High in a tree,
How many blue things
Can you see?

1

I see a blue _____.

5

I see a blue _____ .

2

In my book you will see
☐ blue things.
Do you like blue?
Yes   No

6

I see a blue _____.

3

I read my book to

1. _____

2. _____

3. _____

7

Mary Wore Her Red Dress

Key Concept

Many things can be red.

Preparation

1. Gather theme-appropriate literature.

2. Before using the little book, introduce or reintroduce the color word *red*. Then practice reading the word *red* in context on a chart or in a book.

3. Read or sing *Mary Wore Her Red Dress,* found in the little book.

4. Write the text of the little book on a large chart or prepare an enlarged copy of the little book.

5. Prepare a copy of the little book for each child.

Using the Book

1. Read and review the little book story printed on chart paper. Have children circle the word *red* on the chart.

2. Share a copy of *Mary Wore Her Red Dress* with the class and discuss possible responses. Children may want to make a list of clothing items that could be red. Classmates' names or their own name may be written on the first blank line.

3. Ask children to complete their little books with appropriate words.

4. Provide opportunities for the children to read their completed books to others and utilize the share-and-sign page.

Suggested Literature

Mary Wore Her Red Dress. Nellie Edge Resources, 1988.

Peek, Merle. *Mary Wore Her Red Dress and Henry Wore His Green Sneakers.* Houghton Mifflin, 1993.

Stinson, Kathy. *Red Is Best.* Annick Firefly, 1992.

Mary Wore Her Red Dress

by _____

_____

wore a red _____.

4

Mary Wore Her Red Dress

Traditional Folk Song

1. Mar - y wore her red dress_, red dress_, red dress,

Mar - y wore her red dress_, All day long.

1

_____

wore a red _____.

5

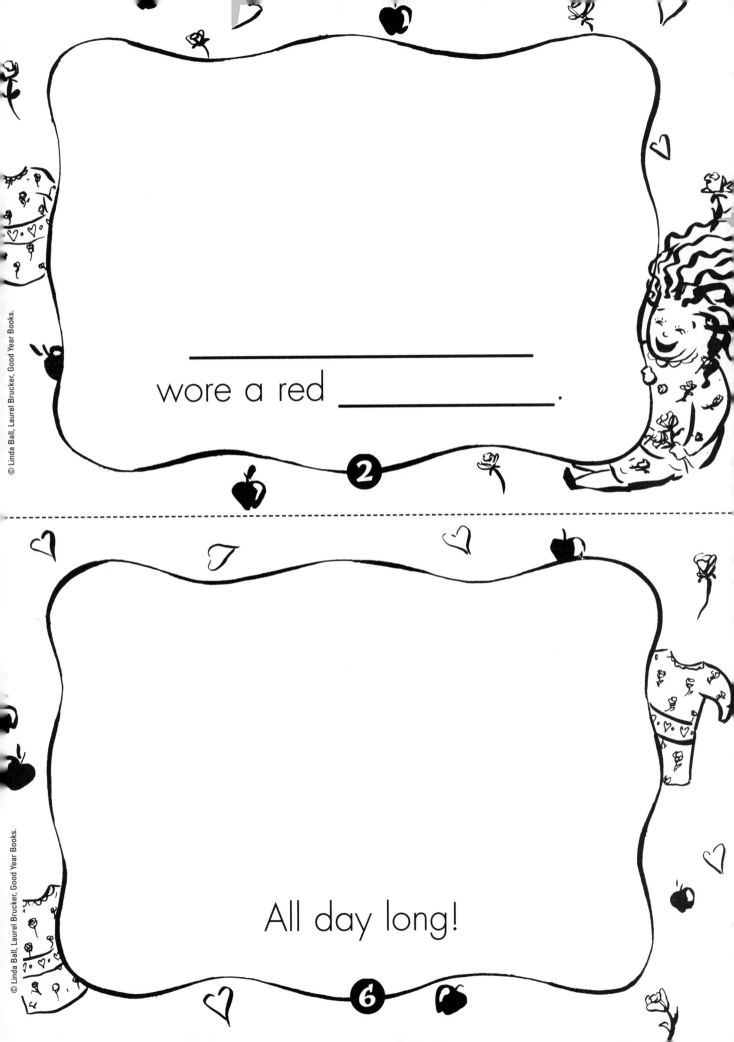

_____
wore a red _____.

2

All day long!

6

_____

wore a red _____.

③

I read my book to

1. _____

2. _____

3. _____

⑦

Teacher's Notes for

I See Colors

Key Concept

Objects can be clas-sified by color.

Preparation

1. Gather theme-appropriate literature.

2. Prepare chart paper for brainstorming by listing the color words found in the book: **Red, Blue, Yellow, Green,** and **Orange.**

3. Prepare a copy of the little book for each child.

Using the Book

1. Read literature selections to the class.

2. Using the prepared chart, brainstorm with the children several things associated with each of the color words listed.

3. Share a copy of *I See Colors* with the class, discussing possible responses.

4. Have children complete their books using ideas from the class chart and their personal vocabularies. On page six of the little book, children should color in the circles to match the color words.

5. Provide opportunities for the children to read their completed books to others and utilize the share-and-sign page.

Suggested Literature

Rossetti, Christina. *Color.* HarperCollins, 1994.

Heller, Ruth. *Color.* Putnam, 1995.

I See Colors

by _____

Green, green, I see a green _____.

4

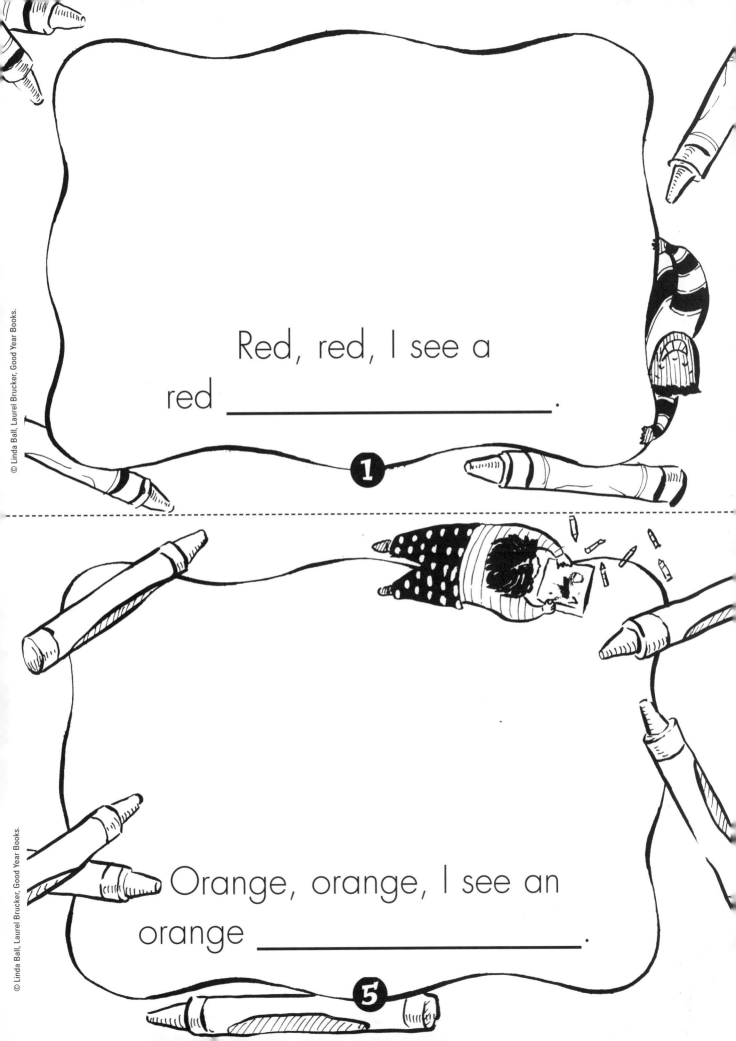

Red, red, I see a
red _____.

1

Orange, orange, I see an
orange _____.

5

Blue, blue, I see a blue _____.

I know my color words:

○ red   ○ blue

○ yellow   ○ green

○ orange

Yellow, yellow, I see a yellow _____.

I read my book to

1. _____

2. _____

3. _____

Teacher's Notes for

The Dot Book

Key Concept

One-to-one correspondence

Preparation

1. Gather theme-appropriate literature.

2. Write the text of the little book on a large chart or prepare an enlarged copy of the little book.

3. Gather manipulatives to allow the children to practice counting.

4. Prepare a copy of the little book for each child.

5. Use colored dot stickers, prepared paper, or colored circles, or allow children to color dots throughout their little books.

Using the Book

1. Read literature selections to the class.

2. Introduce the chart or enlarged copy of the little book.

3. Encourage use of manipulatives and allow children to practice reading or reciting the text and creating pictures using dots.

4. Share a copy of *The Dot Book* with the class, discussing possible responses.

5. Have children complete their books using their own ideas and emphasizing one-to-one correspondence.

6. Provide opportunities for the children to read their completed books to others and utilize the share-and-sign page.

Suggested Literature

Crews, Donald. *Ten Black Dots.* Greenwillow, Inc., 1986.

McGrath, Barbara Barbien. *The M & M's Counting Book.* Charlesbridge Publishing, 1994.

The Dot Book

by _____

With 3 <u>yellow</u> dots I can make

_____.

4

Red dots,
Blue dots,
Yellow dots too.

Green dots,
Many dots,
What can I do?

With 4 <u>green</u> dots I can make

_____.

With 1 <u>red</u> dot I can make

_____.

2

With many dots I can make

_____.

6

With 2 <u>blue</u> dots I can make

_____.

3

I read my book to

1. _____

2. _____

3. _____

7

Section 3

Counting on Math

Teacher's Notes for

Apple Count

Key Concept

Graphing is a way to organize and interpret information.

Preparation

1. Gather theme-appropriate literature.

2. Ask each child to bring an apple to school.

3. Prepare a copy of the little book for each child.

4. Prepare a large, three-column graph for recording the number of apples by color: **Red, Yellow,** and **Green.**

Using the Book

1. Read literature selections to the class.

2. Make a graph, using the apples the children brought to school, by aligning the apples in columns according to color.

3. Pictorially record results of the graph on the prepared written graph.

4. Provide opportunities to count, discuss, and analyze the information from the graph.

5. Share a copy of *Apple Count* with the class, discussing possible responses.

6. Have children complete their books using the information gathered from the graph. On the sixth page of the little book, children should count and record in the box provided.

7. Provide opportunities for the children to read their books to others and utilize the share-and-sign page.

Suggested Literature

Williams, Rozanne Lanczak. *We Can Make Graphs.* Creative Teaching Press, 1995.

Gibbons, Gail. *The Seasons of Arnold's Apple Tree.* Harcourt Brace, 1984.

Apple Count

by _____

How many red? ☐

How many apples
do you see?
Count the apples now with me.

1

Now eat an apple
and go to bed!

5

How many yellow? ▢

2

In my book you will find . . .
▢ yellow apples
▢ green apples
▢ red apples

6

How many green? [   ]

3

I read my book to

1. _____

2. _____

3. _____

7

Teacher's Notes for

Buttons, Buttons

Key Concept

Buttons can be classified by characteristics such as color, shape, size, texture, and quantity.

Preparation

1. Gather theme-appropriate literature.

2. Collect a variety of real buttons and allow the children to explore, sort, and classify the buttons.

3. Provide an assortment of materials for each child to make a button. This button will be used to sort and classify and then will be attached to the sixth page of the little book.

4. Prepare a copy of the little book for each child.

Using the Book

1. Read literature selections to the class.

2. Using the buttons that the children have made, sort and classify in several ways using a variety of attributes. As the children describe the buttons, a list of their descriptive words can be recorded on the board.

3. Share a copy of *Buttons, Buttons* with the class and discuss possible responses.

4. Have each child complete his or her book and glue the button, previously made, on page six.

5. Provide opportunities for the children to read their completed books to others and utilize the share-and-sign page.

Suggested Literature

Williams, Rozanne Lanczak. *Buttons, Buttons.* Creative Teaching Press, 1995.

Reid, Margarette S. *The Button Box.* Puffin Books, 1995.

Buttons, Buttons

by _____

And that's not all.

4

Some buttons are big.

1

My button is _____.
My button is _____.
My button is _____.

5

Some buttons are <u>small</u>.

And it's the best of all!

Some buttons are <u>blue</u>.

I read my book to

1. _____

2. _____

3. _____

In My Home

Key Concept

Counting and number concepts

Preparation

1. Gather theme-appropriate literature.

2. Duplicate the homework page, p.168, and send home with each child.

3. Prepare a copy of the little book for each child.

Using the Book

1. Read literature selections to the class.

2. Collect and discuss homework pages.

3. Share a copy of *In My Home,* demonstrating how the book can be completed using the data from the homework page.

4. Have children complete their books using their personal homework page data.

5. Provide opportunities for the children to read their completed books to others and utilize the share-and-sign page.

Suggested Literature

Brown, Richard. *100 Words About My House.* Live Oak Media, 1990.

Morris, Ann. *Houses and Homes.* Morrow, 1995.

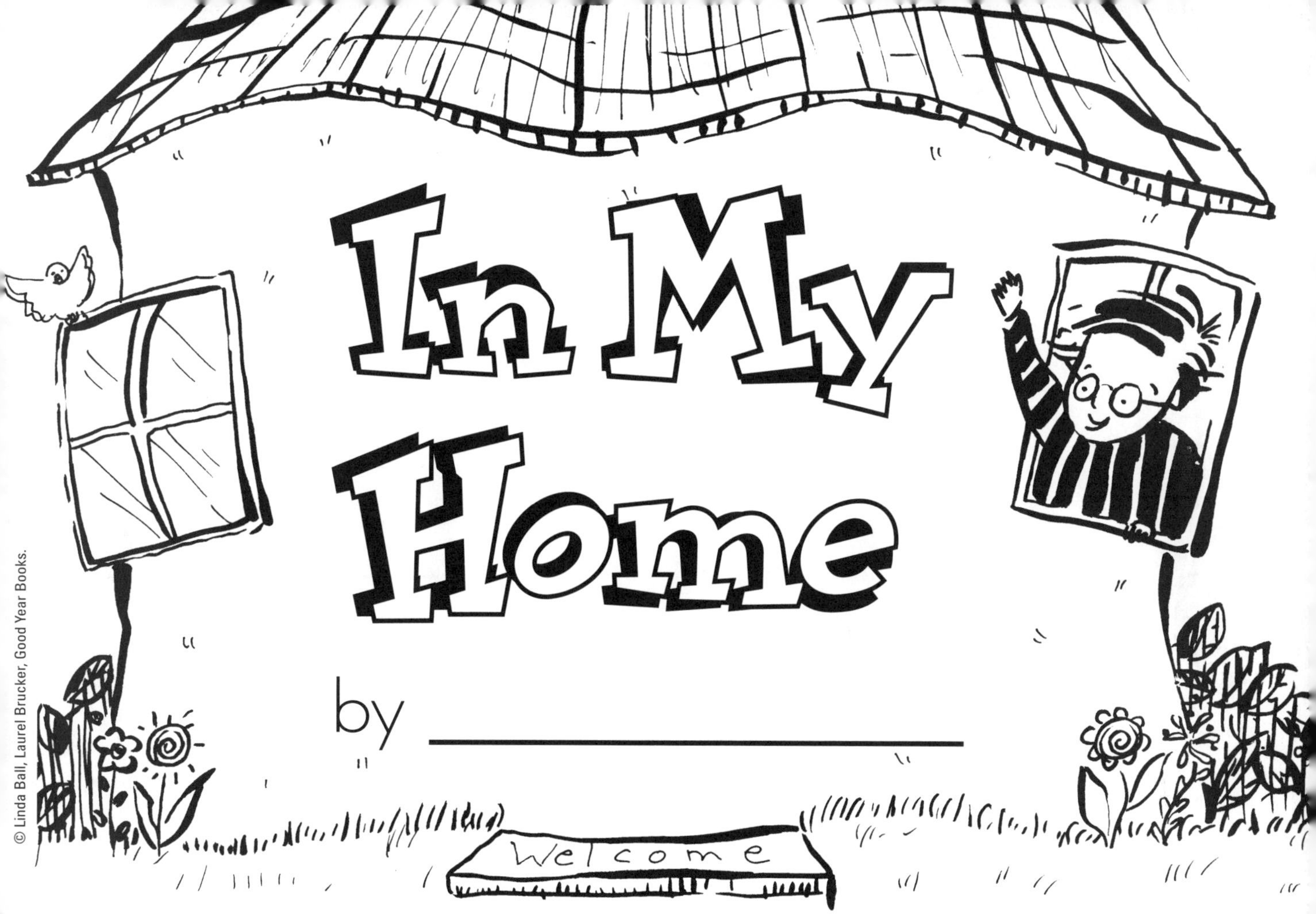

In My Home

by _____

Welcome

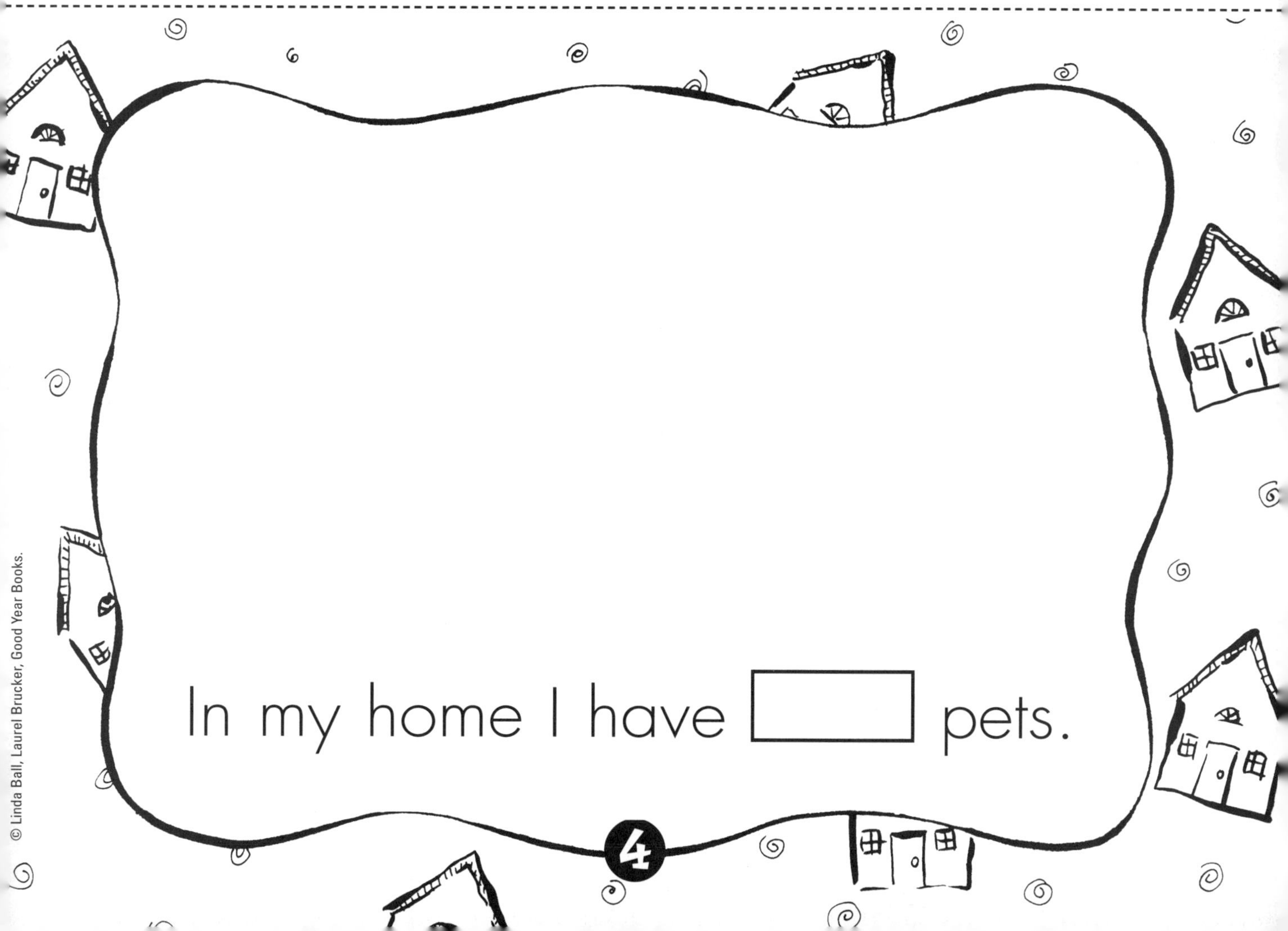

In my home I have ☐ pets.

In my home I have ☐ television sets.

1

In my home I have ☐ people.

5

In my home I have ☐ clocks.

2

In my home, there is me!

6

In my home I have ☐ beds.

3

I read my book to

1. _____

2. _____

3. _____

7

Teacher's Notes for

The Counting Way

Key Concept
Counting and number concepts

Preparation
1. Gather theme-appropriate literature.
2. Provide many counting experiences prior to introducing *The Counting Way* little book.
3. Write the text of the little book on a large chart or prepare an enlarged copy of the little book.
4. Prepare a copy of the little book for each child.

Using the Book
1. Read literature selections to the class.
2. Introduce the chart or enlarged copy of the little book.
3. Discuss possible ways to complete the sentences. Direct children to illustrate each page of their little books and to count and record the appropriate numeral in the boxes provided on the little book pages.
4. Share a copy of *The Counting Way* and ask children to complete their books.
5. Provide opportunities for the children to read their completed books to others and utilize the share-and-sign page.

Suggested Literature
Williams, Rozanne Lanczak. *A-Counting We Will Go*. Creative Teaching Press, 1995.

Anholt, Catherine, and Laurence Anholt. *One, Two, Three, Count with Me*. Puffin, 1996.

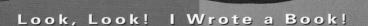

The Counting Way

by _____

I can count <u>green</u> things.

4

I like counting every day.
I'll show you the
counting way.

1

3

I can count

_____ things.

5

I can count <u>big</u> things.

Numbers are fun to say.
How many things
did I count today?

I can count <u>little</u> things.

3

I read my book to

1. _____

2. _____

3. _____

7

How is the Weather?

Mr. Sun

What Shall I Wear?

When It Storms

Rain on the Green Grass

Teacher's Notes for

Mr. Sun

Key Concept

Weather affects what we do.

Preparation

1. Gather theme-appropriate literature.
2. Title two columns of a chart as follows:

    What can you do on a sunny day?

    What can't you do on a sunny day?

3. Write the text of the little book on a large chart or prepare an enlarged copy of the little book.
4. Prepare a copy of the little book for each child.
5. Optional: Ask children to bring in a photo of themselves.

Using the Book

1. Read literature selections to the class.
2. Teach the song "Mr. Sun," pp. 169–170. (See additional resource below.)
3. Using the prepared chart, brainstorm with the class a list of things that can and can't be done on a sunny day.
4. Share a copy of *Mr. Sun* with the class and discuss possible responses.
5. Ask children to complete their books using the words from the chart. Have them either bring a photo or draw a picture of themselves to illustrate page six of the little book.
6. Provide opportunities for the children to read their books to others and utilize the share-and-sign page.

Suggested Literature

Raffi. "Mr. Sun" from *Singable Songs for the Very Young.* A & M Records, 1988.

Tresselt, Alvin. *Sun Up.* Lothrop, 1991.

Mr. Sun

by _____

On a sunny day

I can _____.

Oh, Mr. Sun, Sun,
Mr. Golden Sun,
Please shine down on me.

1

On a sunny day
I can't _____.

5

On a sunny day

I can _____.

❷

Oh, Mr. Sun, Sun, Mr. Golden Sun,
Please shine down on,
Please shine down on,
Please shine down on ME!

❻

On a sunny day
I can _____.

③

I read my book to

1. _____

2. _____

3. _____

⑦

What Shall I Wear?

Key Concept

Weather affects the way we dress.

Preparation

1. Gather theme-appropriate literature.

2. Prepare a chart by titling columns with the types of weather mentioned in the little book (**Cold, Snowy, Hot, Windy,** etc.).

3. Prepare a copy of the little book for each child.

Using the Book

1. Read literature selections to the class.

2. Using the prepared chart, brainstorm with the class what types of clothing are worn in specific kinds of weather.

3. Share a copy of *What Shall I Wear?* with the class, discussing possible responses.

4. Ask children to complete their books using ideas from the chart and their personal vocabularies.

5. Provide opportunities for the children to read their books to others and utilize the share-and-sign page.

Suggested Literature

Neitzel, Shirley. *The Jacket I Wear in the Snow.* William Morrow, 1994.

Borden, Louise. *Caps, Hats, Socks, and Mittens: A Book About the Four Seasons.* Scholastic, 1992.

What Shall I Wear?

by _____

On a snowy, snowy day,
I wear _____.

4

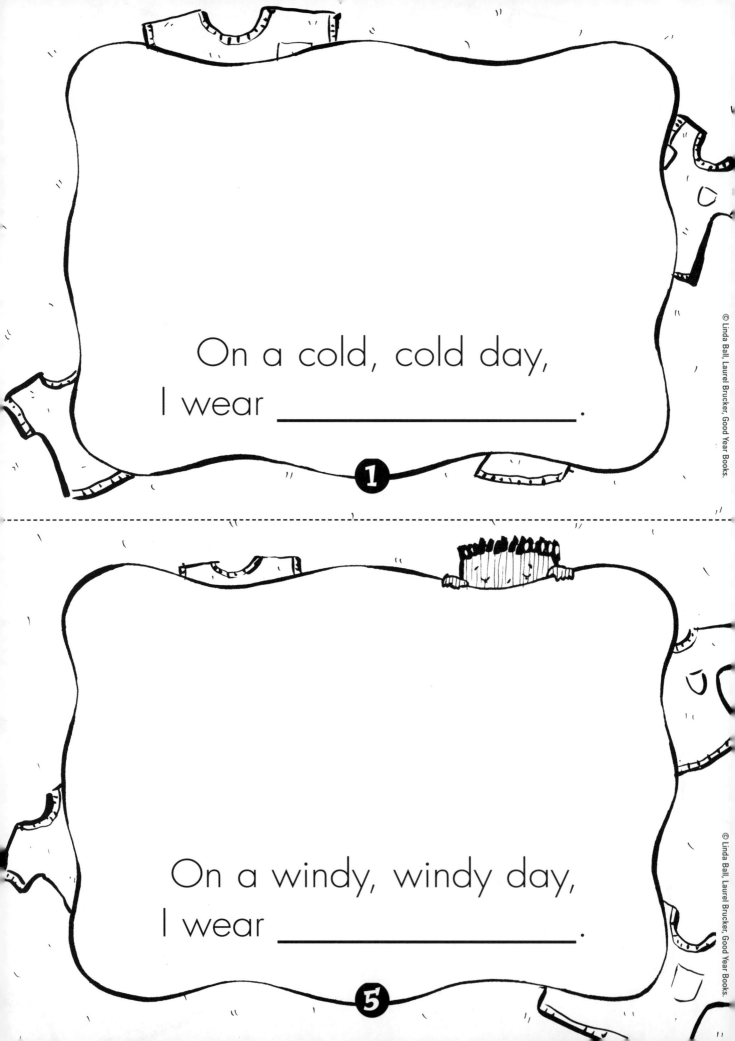

On a cold, cold day,
I wear _____.

1

On a windy, windy day,
I wear _____.

5

On a hot, hot day,
I wear _____.

On a stormy, stormy day,
I stay home!

On a rainy, rainy day,
I wear _____.

I read my book to

1. _____

2. _____

3. _____

Teacher's Notes for

When It Storms

Key Concept
Characteristics of stormy weather

Preparation

1. Gather theme-appropriate literature.

2. Title chart paper as follows:

    When it storms, we see . . .

3. Duplicate the Weather thematic word list, p. 164.

4. Prepare a copy of the little book for each child.

Using the Book

1. Read literature selections to the class.

2. Using the prepared chart, brainstorm with the class a list of the characteristics of a storm.

3. Share a copy of *When It Storms* with the class, discussing possible responses.

4. Have children complete their books using words from the thematic word list, the class chart, and their personal vocabularies. On page six, have children draw a line from the weather word to the matching pictures.

5. Provide opportunities for the children to read their books to others and utilize the share-and-sign page.

Suggested Literature

Leavy, Una. *Harry's Stormy Night.* McElderry Books, 1995.

Polacco, Patricia. *Thunder Cake.* Philomel Books, 1990.

When It Storms

by _____

When it storms,

I see _____.

4

Storm, storm,
Go away.
Come again
another day.
Little __________
wants to play.

When it storms,
I see ____________________.

© Linda Ball, Laurel Brucker, Good Year Books.

When it storms,
I see _____.

2

lightning

rain

clouds

wind

6

When it storms,

I see _____ .

3

I read my book to

1. _____

2. _____

3. _____

7

Teacher's Notes for

Rain on the Green Grass

Key Concept

Rain can fall on many places and things.

Preparation

1. Gather theme-appropriate literature.

2. Write the text of the little book on a large chart or prepare an enlarged copy of the little book. As a variation, each sentence can be written on sentence strips.

3. Prepare a copy of the little book for each child.

Using the Book

1. Read literature selections to the class.

2. Display and read the prepared chart of *Rain on the Green Grass.* Allow children to recite, identifying the word *rain* every time it appears.

3. Discuss places that rain can fall.

4. Share a copy of *Rain on the Green Grass* with the class, discussing possible responses.

5. Have children complete their books.

6. Provide opportunities for the children to read their books to others and utilize the share-and-sign page.

Suggested Literature

Williams, Rozanne Lanczak. *Rain.* Creative Teaching Press, 1995.

Kalan, Robert. *Rain.* Morrow, 1991.

Rain on the Green Grass

by _____

Rain on the _____.

Rain on the green grass,
Rain on the trees.

1

Rain on the _____.

5

Rain on the house top
but not on me.

2

Rain on the _____.
But not on me!

6

Rain on the _____.

3

I read my book to

1. _____

2. _____

3. _____

7

Section 5

Back to Basics

Hello Book

ABC Tumble Down D

School Days

Good Night

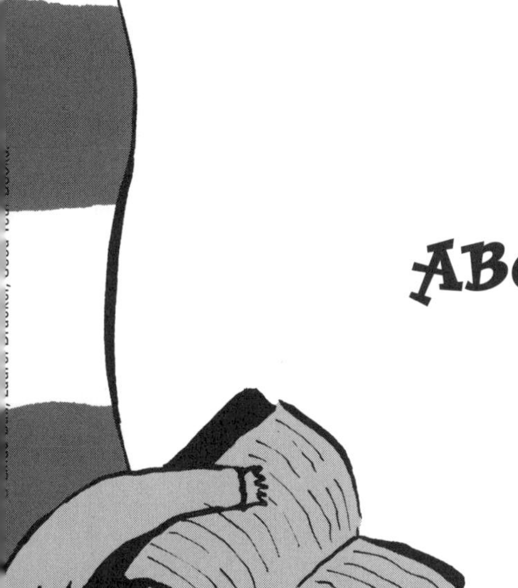

Teacher's Notes for

Hello Book

Key Concept

Becoming familiar with classmates' names

Preparation

1. Gather theme-appropriate literature.

2. Prepare a handwritten class roster as a model for the children to copy.

3. Make a large *Hello Book* for class use. This book has each child's name written on a page.

Hello, Ryan	Hello, Sarah

4. Prepare a copy of the little book for each child.

Using the Book

1. Read literature selections to the class.

2. Read the large *Hello Book* to the class for several weeks. This provides opportunities for children to become familiar with their own names and the names of classmates in print.

3. Introduce the little book to the class and demonstrate how to complete the book using classmates' names.

4. Ask children to complete their books using their classmates' names.

5. Provide opportunities for the children to read their books to others and utilize the share-and-sign page.

Suggested Literature

Lloyd, David. *Hello, Goodbye.* Candlewick Press, 1995.

Aliki. *Hello! Goodbye!* Greenwillow Books, 1996.

Hello   Hola   Bon Jour

Hello

Book

by _____

Shalom   Aloha   Tag   Guten

---

shalom   Hello

Hello,

_____

4

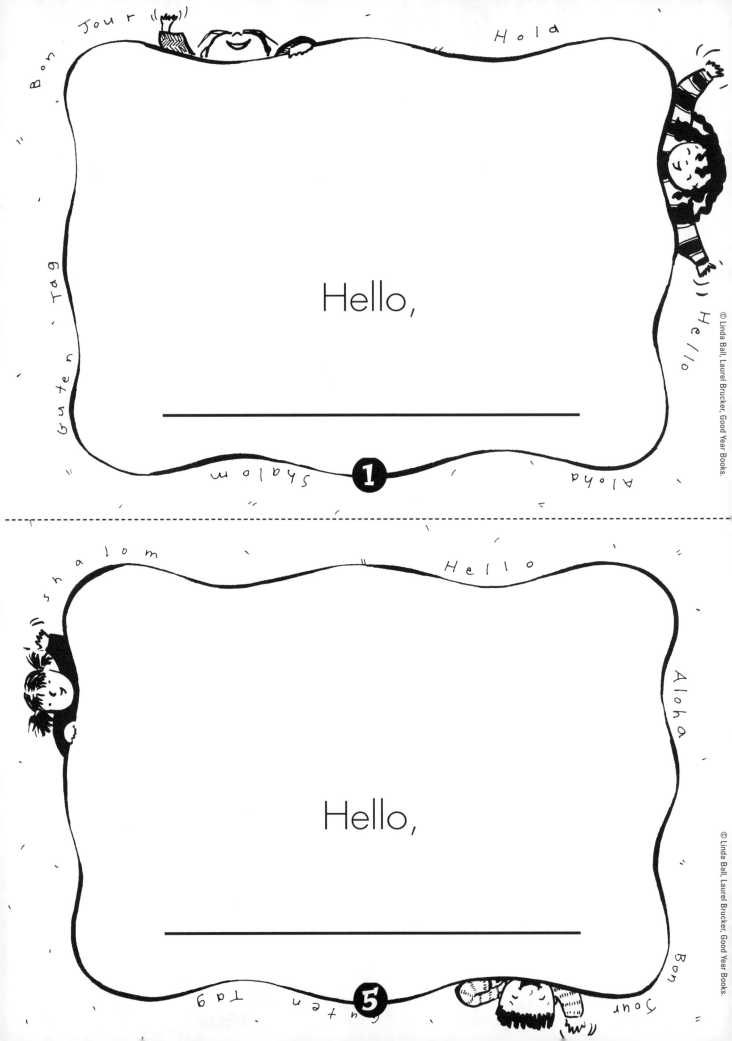

Hello,

_____

1

Hello,

_____

5

Hello,

_____

2

Good-bye,
everyone!

6

Bon Jour

Hola

Guten Tag

Hello

Hello,

_____

③

Shalom

Aloha

I read my book to

1. _____

2. _____

3. _____

⑦

Teacher's Notes for

ABC Tumble Down D

Key Concept

A song can be sung, written, and illustrated.

Preparation

1. Gather theme-appropriate literature.

2. Print the words of the song (found in the little book) on chart paper for classroom display.

3. Prepare a copy of the little book. Provide cat stickers, rubber stamps, or drawings of cats for children to apply to the pages of their little books. They will then be asked to draw an environment around the cats to match the text. As an alternative, you can preprint or stamp a picture of a cat on each page.

Using the Book

1. Read literature selections to the class.

2. Teach the song "ABC Tumble Down D," found on p. 171, to the class, allowing for many opportunities to practice.

3. Use the chart to track the text as the children sing. Record children's responses: The cat's in the _____.

4. Share a copy of the little book *ABC Tumble Down D* with the class, discussing possible responses.

5. Have children complete their books. Ask them to illustrate the cat's location. For example, if a student's response is, "The cat's in the garden," then he or she would draw a garden around the cat.

6. Provide opportunities for the children to read their books to others and utilize the share-and-sign page.

Suggested Literature

Merriam, Eve. *Where Is Everybody?* Simon & Schuster, 1989.

Baker, Alan. *Black and White Rabbit's ABC.* Larousse Kingfisher Chambers, Inc., 1994.

ABC Tumble Down D

by _____

ABC Tumble Down D,
the cat's in the _____
and he can't see me.

ABC Tumble Down D,
the cat's in the cupboard
and he can't see me.

1

ABC Tumble Down D,
the cat's in the _____
and he can't see me.

5

ABC Tumble Down D,
the cat's in the _____
and he can't see me.

ABC Tumble Down D,
the cat's in the _____
and he can't see me.

ABC Tumble Down D,
the cat's in the _____
and he can't see me.

3

I read my book to

1. _____

2. _____

3. _____

7

Teacher's Notes for

School Days

Key Concept

School days are sequential.

Preparation

1.   Gather theme-appropriate literature.

2.   Prepare chart paper or word cards by listing the days of the school week.

3.   Write the school name on a sentence strip.

4.   Duplicate the Things I Do at School thematic word list, p. 165.

5.   Prepare a copy of the little book for each child.

Using the Book

1.   Read literature selections to the class.

2.   Using the prepared chart paper or word cards, discuss the school days, listing things that the children do each day.

3.   Share a copy of *School Days* with the class, discussing possible responses.

4.   Have children complete their books using the ideas from the class list and their personal vocabularies.

5.   Provide opportunities for the children to read their books to others and utilize the share-and-sign page.

Suggested Literature

Ward, Cindy. *Cookie's Week*. Putnam, 1992.

Williams, Rozanne Lanczak. *All Through the Week with Cat and Dog*. Creative Teaching Press, 1995.

School Days

by _____

Thursday, Thursday,
what will I do?
I will _____ at school.

4

Monday, Monday,
what will I do?
I will _____ at school.

1

Friday, Friday,
what will I do?
I will _____ at school.

5

Tuesday, Tuesday,
what will I do?
I will _____ at school.

2

School, school,
this is my school.
The name of my school is

_____.

6

Wednesday, Wednesday,
what will I do?
I will _____ at school.

3

I read my book to

1. _____

2. _____

3. _____

7

Teacher's Notes for

Good Night

Key Concept

Characteristics of day and night are observable.

Preparation

1. Gather theme-appropriate literature.

2. Write the text of the little book on a large chart or prepare an enlarged copy of the little book.

3. Prepare a copy of the little book for each child.

Using the Book

1. Read literature selections to the class.

2. Introduce the chart or enlarged copy of the little book.

3. Share a copy of *Good Night* with the class, discussing possible responses.

4. Have children complete their books using class responses and their personal vocabularies.

5. Provide opportunities for the children to read their books to others and utilize the share-and-sign page.

Suggested Literature

Branley, Franklyn M. *What Makes Day and Night?* HarperCollins, 1986.

Brown, Margaret Wise. *Goodnight Moon.* HarperCollins, 1989.

Good Night

by _____

Good night, _____.

Good night, the moon is in the sky.
Good night, the stars are way up high.
Good night, it's time to go to bed.
Good night, your story
has been read.
Good morning, I see the sun.
Time to get up—the day has begun.

Good night, ________________.

© Linda Ball, Laurel Brucker, Good Year Books.

Good night, _____.

2

Good morning, _____.

6

Good night, _____.

3

I read my book to

1. _____

2. _____

3. _____

7

Living Things

Mrs. Grady's Garden

Key Concept

Many things can grow in a garden.

Preparation

1. Gather theme-appropriate literature.

2. Prepare chart paper for listing of **Fruits** and **Vegetables** that grow in a garden.

3. Duplicate the Gardening thematic word list, p. 166.

4. Prepare a copy of the little book for each child.

Using the Book

1. Read literature selections to the class.

2. Using the prepared chart, brainstorm with the class a list of things that can grow in a garden.

3. Share a copy of *Mrs. Grady's Garden* with the class and discuss possible responses.

4. Have children complete their books using words from the class chart and the thematic word list.

5. Provide opportunities for the children to read their books to others and utilize the share-and-sign page.

Suggested Literature

Caseley, Judith. *Grandpa's Garden Lunch.* Greenwillow Books, 1990.

Pallotta, Jerry, and Bob Thomson. *The Victory Garden Vegetable Alphabet Book.* Charlesbridge Publishing, 1992.

Mrs. Grady's Garden

by _____

These are the _____ that grow in Mrs. Grady's garden.

This is Mrs. Grady.

1

These are the _____
that grow in Mrs. Grady's garden.

5

These are the children who visited Mrs. Grady's garden.

© Linda Ball, Laurel Brucker, Good Year Books.

This is Mrs. Grady's garden. Let's watch it grow and grow and grow.

© Linda Ball, Laurel Brucker, Good Year Books.

These are the _____
that grow in Mrs. Grady's garden.

3

I read my book to

1. _____

2. _____

3. _____

7

Teacher's Notes for

Bug Watch

Key Concept

There are many kinds of bugs, and each bug has unique characteristics.

Preparation

1. Gather theme-appropriate literature.

2. Title chart paper as follows:
   What can bugs do?

3. Duplicate the Bug thematic word list, printed on page six of the little book.

4. Prepare a copy of the little book for each child.

Using the Book

1. Read literature selections to the class.

2. Using the prepared chart, brainstorm with the class a list of things that bugs do.

3. Share a copy of *Bug Watch* with the class and discuss possible responses.

4. Have children complete their books using the words from the class chart and the Bug thematic word list.

5. Provide opportunities for the children to read their books to others and utilize the share-and-sign page.

Suggested Literature

Carle, Eric. *The Very Quiet Cricket*. Philomel Books, 1997.

Sturges, Philemon. *What's That Sound, Woolly Bear?* Little Brown, 1996.

Pallotta, Jerry. *The Icky Bug Alphabet Book*. Charlesbridge, 1991.

Bug Watch

by _____

But all bugs can _____.

4

A _____ can jump.

There are many kinds of bugs.

A _____ can fly.

2

There are many kinds of bugs.

ant

grasshopper

bee

ladybug

spider

caterpillar

6

A _____ can climb.

③

I read my book to

1. _____

2. _____

3. _____

⑦

Teacher's Notes for

What's Alive?

Key Concept

Characteristics of living and nonliving things

Preparation

1. Gather theme-appropriate literature.

2. Title chart paper as follows:
   Living   **Nonliving**

3. Prepare a copy of the little book for each child.

Using the Book

1. Read literature selections to the class.

2. Discuss characteristics of living and nonliving things.

3. Using the prepared chart, brainstorm with the class lists of things that are living or nonliving.

4. Share a copy of *What's Alive?* with the class, discussing possible responses.

5. Have children complete their books using the words from the class chart and their personal vocabularies.

6. Provide opportunities for the children to read their books to others and utilize the share-and-sign page.

Suggested Literature

Graves, Kimberlee. *Is It Alive?* Creative Teaching Press, 1995.

Zoehfeld, Kathleen Weider. *What's Alive?* Let's Read and Find Out Science: HarperCollins, 1995.

What's Alive?

by _____

Is a dish alive?

yes   no

4

All living things need water, food, and air.

Is a fish alive?

yes no

© Linda Ball, Laurel Brucker, Good Year Books.

Is a bear alive?

yes   no

A _____ is alive.
A _____ is not alive.
Are you alive? _____

Is a chair alive?

yes   no

I read my book to

1. _____

2. _____

3. _____

Fish Facts

Key Concept

Fish have distinct characteristics.

Preparation

1. Gather theme-appropriate literature.

2. Title chart paper as follows:

   Fish can: **Fish can't:**

3. Write the text of the little book on a large chart or prepare an enlarged copy of the little book.

4. Prepare a copy of the little book for each child.

Using the Book

1. Read literature selections to the class.

2. Introduce the chart or enlarged copy of the little book. Review it several times before introducing the little book.

3. Using the prepared chart, brainstorm with the class lists of things that fish can do and can't do.

4. Share a copy of *Fish Facts* with the class, discussing possible responses.

5. Have children complete their books using the ideas from the chart and their background knowledge.

6. Provide opportunities for the children to read their books to others and utilize the share-and-sign page.

Suggested Literature

Ehlert, Lois. *Fish Eyes.* Harcourt Brace and Company, 1996.

Fowler, Allan. *It Could Still Be a Fish.* Childrens Press, Inc., 1990.

Fish Facts

by _____

A fish can _____.

1–2–3–4–5
Once I caught a fish alive.

1

A fish can't _____.

5

A fish can _____.

2

6–7–8–9–10
Then I let it go again!

6

A fish can _____.

I read my book to

1. _____

2. _____

3. _____

Family, Friends, and Me

My Favorite Things

Always

Guess Who

See My Family

Teacher's Notes for

My Favorite Things

Key Concept

We are all alike; we are all different.

Preparation

1. Gather theme-appropriate literature.

2. Print the poem "My Favorite Things," p. 171, on chart paper for classroom display.

3. Prepare a copy of the little book for each child.

Using the Book

1. Read literature selections to the class.

2. Read and discuss the poem "My Favorite Things," allowing children to verbalize some of their favorite things.

3. Share a copy of the little book *My Favorite Things* with the class and discuss possible responses.

4. Have children complete their books using their personal vocabularies.

5. Provide opportunities for the children to read their books to others and utilize the share-and-sign page.

Suggested Literature

Anholt, Laurence. *All About You.* Puffin, 1994.

My Favorite Things. (Lyrics/Music). By Rogers and Hammerstein. Illustrated by James Warhola. Simon & Shuster, 1994.

Rockwell, Anne. *What We Like.* Simon & Shuster Children's, 1992.

My Favorite Things

by _____

My favorite food is _____.

4

My favorite color

is ______________________________.

My favorite friend

is ______________________________.

© Linda Ball, Laurel Brucker, Good Year Books.

My favorite animal

is _____.

2

My favorite person
is me, myself, and I.

6

My favorite place to go is _____.

I read my book to

1. _____

2. _____

3. _____

Teacher's Notes for

Always

Key Concept

Children need stability in their lives.

Preparation

1. Gather theme-appropriate literature.

2. Print song text, p. 172, on sentence strips or chart paper. Be sensitive as to whether any of the children no longer have a mother. If so, substitute another word for "Mama" in the song and the little book, leaving several open-ended sentences for children's responses:

   May there always be _____.

3. Prepare a copy of the little book for each child.

Using the Book

1. Read literature selections to the class.

2. Introduce the song "Always" to the class, giving many opportunities for practice.

3. Allow students to respond to the question "What do you wish there always will be?" Record responses on chart paper or sentence strips.

4. Sing "Always" using student responses above.

5. Share a copy of the little book *Always* with the class, discussing possible responses.

6. Have children complete their books using ideas generated by the class and their personal vocabularies.

7. Provide opportunities for the children to read their books to others and utilize the share-and-sign page.

Suggested Literature

Jim Gill Sings the Sneezing Song and Other Contagious Tunes. Jim Gill Music, BMI (P.O. Box 59894, Chicago, IL 60659), 1993.

Sharratt, Nick. *My Mom and Dad Make Me Laugh.* Candlewick Press, 1996.

Always

by _____

May there always

be _____.

May there always be sunshine.
May there always be blue skies.

1

May there always

be _____.

5

May there always be Mama.
May there always be me.

2

May there always be me.

6

May there always

be _____.

I read my book to

1. _____

2. _____

3. _____

teacher's notes for

Guess Who

Key Concept

People can be classified according to personal attributes.

Preparation

1. Gather theme-appropriate literature.

2. Prepare sentence strips and laminate them. Then play the attribute guessing game described below. Here are some examples of sentence strips:

   I have _____ eyes.

   I have _____ hair.

   I like to _____.

   I am a _____.

3. Prepare a copy of the little book for each child.

Using the Book

1. Read literature selections to the class.

2. Discuss personal attributes of students.

3. Display sentence strips. List students' responses on each strip.

4. Play an attribute guessing game. First, all children stand, and then the teacher reads a sentence strip filling in one attribute. If the attribute does not pertain to a student, he or she sits down. Continue with other sentence strips until one student remains standing.

5. Share a copy of *Guess Who?* with the class, discussing possible responses.

6. Have children complete their books using class responses and their personal vocabularies.

7. Provide opportunities for the children to read their books to others and utilize the share-and-sign page.

Suggested Literature

Maguire, Arlene. *We're All Special.* Portanus Publishing, 1995.

Carson, Nancy. *I Like Me.* Puffin, 1993.

Guess Who?

by _____

I like to _____.

I have ______________ eyes.

1

I am a ______________.

5

© Linda Ball, Laurel Brucker, Good Year Books.

I have _____ hair.

2

My name is _____.

6

I like to _____.

3

I read my book to

1. _____

2. _____

3. _____

7

Teacher's Notes for

See My Family

Key Concept

A family is a special group of people.

Preparation

1. Gather appropriate literature about families.

2. Make an enlarged copy of the little book and complete using your family information.

3. Duplicate the Family thematic word list, p. 167.

4. Prepare a copy of the little book for each child.

Using the Book

1. Read literature selections to the class.

2. Discuss how families are alike and different.

3. Share the teacher's enlarged copy of *See My Family* with the class. Encourage discussion of the teacher's family book.

4. Share a copy of the little book *See My Family* with the class and discuss possible responses.

5. Have children complete their books using words from the thematic word list and their personal vocabularies.

6. Provide opportunities for the children to read their books to others and utilize the share-and-sign page.

Suggested Literature

Pellegrini, Nina. *Families Are Different*. Holiday House, 1991.

Hoberman, Mary Ann. *Mr. and Mrs. Muddle*. Joy Street Books, 1988.

See My Family

by _____

Here is my _____.

See my family,
See them all.
Some are short.
Some are tall.

1

Here is my family.

5

Here is my _____.

2

Sometimes happy,
Sometimes sad.
We love each other,
And I am glad!

6

Here is my _____.

3

I read my book to

1. _____

2. _____

3. _____

7

Appendix

- **Fall Words List**

- **Winter Words List**

- **Spring Words List**

- **Things I do at School Words List**

- **Gardening Words List**

- **A Family Words List**

- **The Counting House—Homework**

- **"Mr. Sun" song**

- **"ABC Tumble Down D" song**

- **"My Favorite Things" poem**

- **"Always" song**

- **Letter to Parents**

- **Student Assessment Form**

Fall Words

pumpkin

squirrel

tree

scarecrow

leaf

Halloween

apple

acorn

trick or treat

jack-o'-lantern

I like fall!

Winter Words

coat

scarf

boots

mittens

hat

snow

ice

snowman

skates

sled

I like winter!

Spring Words

kite

butterfly

fly

flower

sun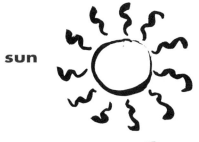

bug

rain

bird

wind

nest

I like spring!

Weather Words

sun

snow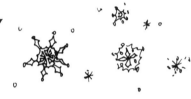

rain

fog

wind

lightning

clouds

hot — cold

thermometer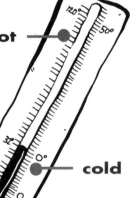

Things I do at School

play

eat

read

listen

work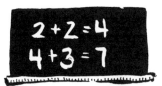

build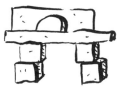

paint

count

write

sing

Gardening

plant

flower

seeds

leaf

bulb

stem

sun

roots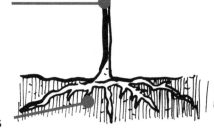

water

garden

dirt

worm

A Family

mom    dad

stepmom    stepdad

sister    brother

grandma    grandpa

baby    pet

Homework   Name _____

The Counting House

In my home I have—

☐ television sets

 ☐ clocks

☐ beds

 ☐ pets

 ☐ people

Please complete with your child and return on _____.
Thank you!

Look, Look! I Wrote a Book!

Mr. Sun

Medium fast (Whistle 2nd time) Traditional

Oh Mis - ter Sun, Sun, Mis - ter Gol - den Sun,

please shine down on me. Oh Mis - ter Sun, Sun,

Mis - ter Gold - en Sun, hid - ing be - hind a tree.

These lit - tle chil - dren are ____ ask - ing you to please come out so we can

(Continued on next page)

(Continued from previous page)

play with you. Oh Mis - ter Sun, Sun, Mis - ter Gold - en Sun,

please shine down on me. Oh Mis - ter please shine down on,

please shine down on, please shine down on, me.

ABC Tumble Down D

A- B- C- Tum - ble down D. The cat's in the cup-board and he can't see me.

C G C | C G C G₇ | C C G₇ G₇ | C G₇ C

My Favorite Things

I like red,
I like blue,
I like pink and purple too.

I like pizza,
I like cakes,
I like anything my mom bakes.

I like birds,
I like frogs,
I like big and friendly dogs.

I like Sarah,
I like Dan,
I like my best friend named Jan.

I like swings,
I like bikes,
I like going on long hikes.

I like pumpkins,
I like pie,
I like me, myself, and I.

written by Linda Ball and Laurel Brucker

Look, Look! I Wrote a Book!

Always

traditional folk song

May there   al - ways be   sun - shine. May there

al - ways be   blue skies.   May there

al - ways be Ma - ma. May there al - ways be me!

Dear Parents:

The children are bringing home their first collection of little books. They will continue to make and collect the little books throughout the school year. We have provided a decorated container for each child to store her or his books in at home. Please find a special place for this container so that your child can continue to read the books and add to her or his collection as we complete more books.

We feel that the little books are a very important part of our reading/writing program. The books have been personalized by your child as an author and illustrator. Your child has had successful reading experiences with other children and adults, as evidenced by the list of names on the last page of each book. Please take time to read the books with your child and add your signature to the back page of each book.

Little books provide your child with opportunities to "read" at the various stages of reading development:

1. Enjoys the story

2. Can memorize parts or all of the story

3. Can retell the story

4. Can recognize some words in the story

5. Can read some or all of the words with accuracy

It is very important that your child experience success as she or he reads the books. Many children are unable to read the books word for word at this point. Please praise all efforts and encourage frequent reading.

We hope that you enjoy the little books!

Sincerely,

Name _____ Date _____

Student Assessment

1. Can the child choose a specific book from the collection? _____
_____

2. Can the child model proper reading behaviors?
_____

3. Can the child follow the print? _____
_____

4. Can the child locate a specific word or phrase?
_____

5. Can the child read the text accurately? _____
_____

Comments: